live it
learn it

BIBLE STUDIES

PRAYER

Group
Loveland, Colorado

Group's R.E.A.L. Guarantee to you:

This Group resource incorporates our R.E.A.L. approach to ministry—one that encourages long-term retention and life transformation. It's ministry that's:

Relational
Because learner-to-learner interaction enhances learning and builds Christian friendships.

Experiential
Because what learners experience through discussion and action sticks with them up to 9 times longer than what they simply hear or read.

Applicable
Because the aim of Christian education is to equip learners to be both hearers and doers of God's Word.

Learner-based
Because learners understand and retain more when the learning process takes into consideration how they learn best.

Learn It, Live It Bible Studies™: Prayer
Copyright © 2003 Group Publishing, Inc.

Visit our Web site: **www.grouppublishing.com**

All rights reserved. No part of this book may be reproduced in any manner whatsoever without prior written permission from the publisher, except where noted in the text and in the case of brief quotations embodied in critical articles and reviews. For information, write Permissions, Group Publishing, Inc., Dept. PD, P.O. Box 481, Loveland, CO 80539.

Credits
Contributors: Stacey Campbell, Tracey D. Lawrence, and Keith Madsen
Editor: Beth Rowland
Development Editor: Matt Lockhart
Chief Creative Officer: Joani Schultz
Copy Editor: Lyndsay E. Gerwing
Art Director: Randy Kady
Cover Art Director: Jeff A. Storm
Cover Designer: Toolbox Creative
Cover Photographer: Daniel Treat
Print Production Artist: Susan Tripp
Production Manager: Dodie Tipton

Unless otherwise noted, Scripture taken from the HOLY BIBLE, NEW INTERNATIONAL VERSION®. Copyright © 1973, 1978, 1984 by International Bible Society. Used by permission of Zondervan Publishing House. All rights reserved.

ISBN 0-7644-2668-0

10 9 8 7 6 5 4 3 2 1   12 11 10 09 08 07 06 05 04 03

Printed in the United States of America.

Table of Contents

Introduction 4

About the Sessions 6

   Session 1: Praise 9

   Session 2: Thanksgiving 19

   Session 3: Confession 29

   Session 4: Petition 39

   Session 5: Intercession 49

   Session 6: Listening to God 59

   Session 7: The Lord's Prayer 71

Introduction to Group's
Learn It, Live It Bible Studies™

Welcome to an exciting new concept in small-group Bible studies! At Group, we recognize the value of Bible study to Christian growth—there's no better way to grow in our faith than to study the living Word of God. We also know the value of group activity. Activity helps us practice what we learn. And this is vital to the Christian faith. Jesus doesn't tell us simply to learn about him; he asks us to become like him in thoughts, in words, and in actions. That's why Group developed *Learn It, Live It Bible Studies*™. In these studies, you'll be challenged not only to learn more about God but also to put what you've learned into practice in a powerful and meaningful way.

Whether you're new to Bible study or a seasoned pro, you'll find each lesson's Bible study to be interesting and compelling. You'll open God's Word with the others in your group. You'll study relevant Scripture passages and discuss thought-provoking questions that will help you all grow in your faith and in your understanding of who God is and what he wants for your lives.

After the Bible study, you'll be invited to choose a group project that will help you practice the very thing you've just learned. Some of these projects are simple, easy, and low-risk. Others will require a greater commitment of time and resources; they may even take you beyond your comfort zone. But whichever group project you choose to do, you can be certain that it will help you grow more like Christ in your everyday life.

We hope you enjoy these lessons! And we pray that by studying these lessons and doing these projects, you'll find yourself becoming more and more like our Lord Jesus Christ.

Prayer

This seven-session Bible study focuses on prayer, the communication we have with God. As God's children, Christians have the opportunity to talk to the Almighty Creator of the universe whenever we wish. Hebrews tells us that because of Christ's death and resurrection we can approach the throne of God with confidence! There is no barrier between God and us.

Despite this amazing privilege, Christians too often don't take advantage of the opportunity to seek counsel with an all-knowing, all-wise God. Sometimes we fear that God will lead us in a direction we don't want to go. Sometimes we are too ashamed of our sins and imperfections to face a holy God. Sometimes we are simply too busy directing our own lives to submit to an all-powerful Lord. And sometimes we just don't know what to say to a God we can't see and have trouble understanding.

These seven lessons will demystify prayer and help you appreciate the beauty and privilege of conversation with God. You'll learn what Scripture has to say about prayer, and you'll find plenty of opportunities to practice different kinds of prayer individually and as a group.

About the Sessions

Part 1: learn it

Start It (15 minutes)

This part of the lesson is designed to introduce everyone to the day's topic and to get your discussion flowing. Here you'll find an introduction to read over and a quick warm-up to do together.

Study It (45-60 minutes)

This is the Bible study portion of the lesson. Every lesson provides several Scripture passages to look up and nine to twelve discussion questions for you to talk over as a group. Feel free to jot down your insights in the space provided.

You'll also notice that each lesson includes extra information in the margins. You'll find Bible facts, definitions, and quotations. Please note that the information doesn't always come from a Christian perspective. These margin notes are meant to be thought-provoking and to get your group discussing each topic at a deeper level.

Close It (15-30 minutes)

During the Close It section of the lesson, you'll do two things. First you'll read through the Live It options at the end of the lesson and choose one to do together as a group. You'll find more information about the Live It options in the next section.

Second, you'll pray together as a group. Be sure to take the time to listen to one another's prayer requests. You may want to write those prayer requests in the space provided so you can pray for those requests throughout the week. Don't rush your time with God. Praying with others is a precious opportunity—make the most of it!

Part 2: live it

In each lesson in this study, you'll find five Live It options. These group activities are designed to help your Bible study group live out what you learned in the Bible study. Together as a group, read over the Live It options each week. Then choose one to do together. You'll find that some of the activities are quick and easy and can be done easily without planning an extra session, while other activities will require more time and planning. Some activities are very low-risk; others might push group members to the edge of their comfort zone. Some of the activities are suitable for entire families to participate in; others will work better if you arrange for child care. Choose the option that interests your group the most and carry it out. You'll find that you learn so much more when you practice it in real life.

SESSION 1

Praise

Prayer is designed to keep us in constant communion with God, and praise is a vital part of our relationship to God. Scripture is full of praise and adoration to God. Angels give praise to God. Israel praises God in the Hallel (or hallelujah) Psalms*. Scripture encourages everything that has breath to praise God. Even nature praises God!

Prayers of praise and thanksgiving are closely related and many times run together in our communication with God. In praise we are acknowledging and appreciating the glory, wonder, and magnificence of our God. We praise God for who he is, rather than just what he has done for us. Our focus is more on God's complete "otherness" than it is on matters of life on earth. This focus gives us a more balanced view of ourselves and the world in which we live.

In this lesson, we will look at the importance of praise in our prayer life. When we meditate upon God and recount his blessings, prayers of praise will be seen as both a duty and a delight. Through praise and worship, our calling and purpose as God's children is more fully realized. Praising God deepens our communion with God—we are able to forget about ourselves and focus solely on him. This lesson will illustrate what is stated in the *Westminster Catechism*: "Man's chief end is to glorify God and enjoy him forever."

*Psalms 113-118

Part 1: learn it

Start It *(15 minutes)*
Reasons to Praise

> Leader: This is the start of a new study series or perhaps even the beginning of your small group. Take the opportunity to help the members of your group discuss their expectations for the series and the relationships in the group. You might even consider having your group draft a list of expectations for the group, such as attendance and how long you'll meet.

To get the session started, recall a time in your life when you were praised for something. Tell the group what happened and how you felt when you were praised.

Then discuss this question:

- **How do you think God feels when we praise him?**

Next, reflect on your personal prayer life. List five reasons that you find it is easy to praise God and five reasons it is difficult at times. Share your lists with the rest of the group.

1.	1.
2.	2.
3.	3.
4.	4.
5.	5.

Study It *(45-60 minutes)*

> If you have a large group, form smaller groups of four to seven people to answer the discussion questions. At the end of the Study It section, allow time for the subgroups to report to the whole group.

1. How would you describe your perspective about praising God? Is praise a duty? a joy? a privilege? a trust? a chore? What makes you feel the way you do about praising God?

2. What does it mean to praise God?

Read Revelation 5:11-14.

3. Why is God worthy of praise?

> "Prayer of praise is devoted directly to God for His own sake apart from anything we may or may not have received from Him."
>
> **Henri Nouwen**

Read what Henri Nouwen said about praise.

4. Do you agree with Nouwen? Why or why not?

5. Why do we praise God? Does God need us to praise him? Why or why not?

Read 2 Chronicles 20:2-30.

6. Why did Jehoshaphat and his army praise God? What was the result of praising God?

7. How does praising God affect our lives, our attitudes, and our relationship with God?

8. Read the following Scriptures about praise. Divide the Scriptures among pairs and trios in the group. Have the pairs and trios note what they learn about praise. Then have them report their insights back to the group.
   - *Deuteronomy 8:10*
   - *1 Chronicles 15:1; 16:4-6*
   - *Job 1:21*
   - *Psalm 34:1*
   - *Psalm 113:2-3*
   - *2 Corinthians 1:3-5*
   - *Hebrews 13:15*
   - *1 Peter 2:9*
   - *1 Peter 4:11*

> Here are some other words that appear in the Bible as synonyms of the word *praise*.
> - *bless*
> - *magnify*
> - *extol*
> - *exalt*
> - *laud*
> - *glorify*

Read the margin note about synonyms for the word praise, *and consider the shades of meaning of each word. You may want to consult a dictionary.*

9. How does the meaning of these different words enhance your understanding of what it means to praise God?

10. What can you do to make praise a regular part of your prayer life?

Close It *(15-30 minutes)*

Review the options in the Live It section of this session and make plans as a group to complete one of these activities prior to moving on to the next session. This is your opportunity to move from theory to practice—*carpe diem!*

Pray It

Share prayer requests, and close in prayer. Be sure to ask God to guide your efforts as you plan and carry out a Live It activity.

Plan It

What activity are we going to do?

When are we doing this?

Where will this take place?

Other: special instructions/my responsibility

Part 2: live it

Option 1

Meet together and take turns reading aloud Psalms 113–118, the "Egyptian Hallel." In Bible times, families chanted these psalms during the feast of Passover. Read each psalm aloud, then pause to let people pray their own prayers of praise either silently or out loud. You may want to make this a joyful yet reverent time of praise by turning out all the lights and praying by the light of candles. You may also want to play quiet praise music in the background.

Option 2

Search your Bibles as a group, and see how many different names you can come up with for God. What names mean the most to you? What names have you not thought about before? Then incorporate those names of God into a time of praise. Divide the list of names among the people in the group. Take turns having each person pray, "We praise you, Lord, for being..." and fill in the blank with the name of God. For example, the person might pray, "We praise you, Lord, for being a consuming fire." Then pause to allow people to silently praise God for how he has revealed himself as the consuming fire. Then move on to the next name.

Option 3

Take time as a group to praise God for the attributes he alone possesses. Think for a moment what life would be like if we possessed such attributes. As finite creatures, we would not be able to steward such power. While playing God might be fun for a day, *being* God is another matter altogether.

Read the following Scriptures that describe God's unique attributes. Then spend time in prayer, praising God for his uniqueness.

God is omniscient—Job 37:16; Isaiah 46:9-10; 1 John 3:20.
God is omnipresent—Psalm 90:2; Psalm 139:7; Revelation 1:8.
God is omnipotent—1 Chronicles 29:12; Matthew 19:26; Luke 8:25.

God is immutable—Numbers 23:19; Psalm 33:11; Psalm 102:25-27; James 1:17.

God is eternal—Deuteronomy 33:27; Psalm 145:13; Revelation 1:8.

Option 4

Attend a Christian concert together. Choose a concert by a group known for playing music that praises God. If there aren't any Christian concerts in your area, attend a song service or a praise and worship service at a church in your area that has a different style of worship than your church does. Enjoy praising God together.

Option 5

Declare one day this week to be a day of praise. Have group members agree to consciously praise God from the moment they wake up that morning until the moment they fall asleep that night. Have everyone consider during the day the things God has done that are praiseworthy, along with praising God simply for who he is.

Debrief It

After experiencing this session's Live It activity, discuss these questions as a group:

- **On a scale of 1 (low) to 10 (high), how would you rank this experience for yourself? Why?**

- **What was the most important insight you gained from this experience?**

- **How can you incorporate this kind of prayer into your life regularly?**

Journal It

The following space is provided for you to record your personal thoughts, reflections, impressions, or feelings about this session's topic and Live It activity.

SESSION 2: Thanksgiving

Being thankful is an important part of our culture. One of the first things we teach our children is to say "thank you" when others are kind to them or give them presents. We know the importance of sending thank you notes for gifts. We even have a national holiday to celebrate our gratefulness for our blessings.

Even so, it's easy to forget to express our thanks to the One who deserves it most. As Christians, we are to be thankful people. Scripture is full of admonitions to thank God. And if we spend even the smallest bit of time reflecting on God's character and his actions toward us, we are bound to be overflowing with thanks to our Father in heaven.

Thanksgiving is an integral part of prayer. Thanksgiving is acknowledging and being glad for what God does. It is the humble admission that all we have comes from God and not from anything we do ourselves. To be a thankful person is to be grateful to God in all circumstances, even difficult ones.

This lesson will help you explore what it means to be a thankful Christian. It will also provide you with the opportunity to tell God exactly why you're grateful for him.

Part 1: learn it

Start It *(15 minutes)*
Thank You Notes

> **Leader Note:** You'll need to provide a note card and envelope for each person.

On the note card your leader provides, write a quick thank you note to someone who has done something kind for you in the last month.

Then tell the group who you wrote the note for and what that person did for you.

Together, discuss these questions:

- **How does it feel to send a thank you note?**

- **How does it feel to receive a thank you note?**

- **Why is expressing thanks so important?**

Study It *(45-60 minutes)*

> If you have a large group, form smaller groups of four to seven people to answer the discussion questions. At the end of the **Study It** section, allow time for the subgroups to report to the whole group.

1. What role does being thankful play in our culture?

2. Why is giving thanks to God important for Christians? What does giving thanks remind us about God and ourselves?

Read the information in the margin.

3. Do Christians give thanksgiving the importance it deserves? Explain.

> Giving thanks was so important to the Jews in Bible times that it was among the official, priestly duties of the Levites. See 1 Chronicles 16:4 and 1 Chronicles 23:28-31.

4. Is thanksgiving a priority in your life? Tell the group how giving thanks has affected your life.

5. Read the following passages. What do you learn from Paul's expressions of thanks?

- *Romans 1:8*
- *1 Corinthians 1:4-5*
- *Philippians 1:3-6*
- *Colossians 1:3-6*
- *1 Thessalonians 1:2-3*
- *2 Thessalonians 1:3*
- *2 Timothy 1:3*
- *Philemon 4-5*

Read Luke 17:11-19; Romans 1:21; and 2 Timothy 3:1-2.

6. What can you learn from these examples of ingratitude?

7. What happens when we neglect to give thanks to God?

Read Psalm 69:30-31.

8. Why does God value thankfulness more than sacrifice?

9. Read the following passages and write down what you learn about giving thanks. You may want to form pairs and divide the passages among the pairs. Allow time for each pair to share its insights with the rest of the group.

- *2 Corinthians 9:11-15*
- *Ephesians 4:2*
- *Ephesians 5:19-20*
- *Philippians 4:6*
- *Colossians 2:6-7*
- *1 Thessalonians 5:16-18*
- *1 Timothy 4:3-5*
- *Hebrews 12:28-29*

10. How would becoming a person characterized by gratitude affect your character, your outlook on life, your attitude toward others, and your relationship with God?

Close It *(15-30 minutes)*

Review the options in the Live It section of this session, and make plans as a group to complete one of these activities prior to moving on to the next session. This is your opportunity to move from theory to practice—*carpe diem!*

Pray It

Share prayer requests, and close in prayer. Be sure to ask God to guide your efforts as you plan and carry out a Live It activity.

Plan It

What activity are we going to do?

When are we doing this?

Where will this take place?

Other: special instructions/my responsibility

Part 2: live it

Option 1

In Bible times, the Israelites built altars to help them remember what God had done for them. Have each person, couple, or family in your group work together to build something to remember what God has done for them. Then gather and have each person, couple, or family present what they made and explain what it commemorates. Have a time of thanksgiving, and thank God together for his gracious and mighty deeds among us.

Option 2

Plan to spend an evening giving thanks to God. Gather and pray corporately for at least an hour. Make it a point not to ask God for anything but to simply give thanks for all that he has done and is.

Option 3

Create a Thanksgiving book. Purchase an inexpensive scrapbook. Have each person, couple, or family take turns putting items in the scrapbook that remind them of things God has done for them for which they are thankful. Have each person, couple, or family show their scrapbook pages to the group before turning the book over to the next person. When everyone has had a chance to contribute to the book, spend time looking at the book together and giving thanks to God in prayer for the many things he has done for all of you.

Option 4

Get together one evening. Form groups of two or three, and have each pair or trio do one of the following projects to express its thanks to God:
- write a poem,
- write a song,
- draw a picture, or
- create a skit.

Have each pair or trio present its project to the rest of the group. Between presentations, encourage one another to thank God in silent or corporate prayer.

Option 5

Celebrate a traditional Thanksgiving feast together. Split the cooking duties among the group members. During the meal, talk about what God has done for you. Be sure to begin your feast with a prayer of thanksgiving. Then end your feast by spending time in prayer together, and have each person give thanks to God.

Debrief It

After experiencing this session's Live It activity, discuss these questions as a group:

- **On a scale of 1 (low) to 10 (high), how would you rank this experience for yourself? Why?**

- **What was the most important insight you gained from this experience?**

- **How can you incorporate this kind of prayer into your life regularly?**

The following space is provided for you to record your personal thoughts, reflections, impressions, or feelings about this session's topic and Live It activity.

SESSION 3

Confession

It is said that confession is good for the soul. Why, then, do people in our time seem to have so much difficulty with it? Politicians "cross the line" in some area of behavior, and instead of confessing, they speak of "plausible deniability" and bring out their "spin doctors" to make their mistakes or sins look like something far more benign. But this is not just a problem with politicians.

Most of us have a strong aversion to admitting our flaws and failures. We can't control our anger, but instead of confessing the weakness, we blame the rest of the world for "making us mad." We buy far more than we need, and instead of confessing to our own greed, we blame our society for being "too commercial." Certainly all complex problems have many contributing factors, but why is it so difficult to confess that at least part of the problem is us? It's hard! We do so want to think of ourselves as competent, good people!

Confession is tough because it is brutal honesty. It's coming clean before God, admitting to him exactly the kind of people we really are. And since we know what kind of people we really are, that's tough to do. But the good news is that God already knows what we're really like. Confessing to God doesn't give God any more information about us than he already has. And God loves us—flaws, doubts, and all!

God wants us to be open and honest with him. Confession increases our intimacy with him, and it increases our dependence on him. God wants us to confess where we fall short of what we should be—that's how we recognize how much we need his presence in our lives. This lesson will help you to find the importance of confession in prayer and how such confession can free up the rest of your life.

Part 1: *learn it*

Start It *(15 minutes)*
"Lite" Confessions

Have someone read aloud the following list of questions one at a time. Have group members stand up to "confess" that they've committed that "offense."

- Have you ever gone skinny-dipping in a river, ocean, lake, or farm pond?

- Have you ever gone to a grocery store mainly to eat the free samples?

- Have you ever let the answering machine screen your calls even though you were home?

- Have you ever stuck your used chewing gum on the underside of a public table?

- Have you ever drunk right out of the milk or juice carton and put it back in the refrigerator?

- Have you ever sneaked into a drive-in movie?

- Have you ever called someone and then forgotten who it was you had called?

- Have you ever had a conversation with someone at church and tried to cover up the fact that you had totally forgotten his or her name?

Next, choose one or two of the following questions to answer and share with the group:

- How do you feel when you have to confess to something? Does it make it easier if it's something silly like one of the questions above? Explain.

- When you were a child or teenager, how likely were your parents to admit to you when they were wrong? How did you feel about this?

- When you were a teenager, what was the hardest thing you ever had to confess to your parents?

Study It *(45-60 minutes)*

> If you have a large group, form smaller groups of four to seven people to answer the discussion questions. At the end of the Study It section, allow time for the subgroups to report to the whole group.

1. Read each of the following statements. Discuss whether you agree or disagree with each of them. If possible, use Scripture passages you're familiar with to support your opinions.

    - **A Christian's daily sins aren't forgiven until they're confessed.**

    - **Confessing our sins makes us closer to God.**

    - **Confessing our sins increases God's favor toward us.**

    - **It's just as important to confess to other Christians as it is to confess to God.**

    - **Confessing as a group (nation, church, or family) is important and effective.**

Read I Kings 8:33-36; Nehemiah 1:5-9; Proverbs 28:13; and I John 1:9.

2. What is the purpose of confession?

Read the quote from Manfred Koehler. Also read Psalm 32:3-5.

> "Some of the burdens I had carried for so long seemed to disappear [when I confessed]. I sensed God was neither angry nor surprised by my confession. On the contrary, He had patiently waited to hear from my own lips what He knew to be true all along."
>
> **Manfred Koehler,** "The Freedom of Confession," Discipleship Journal

3. What emotions do people experience before and after confessing to God? Why do we experience those emotions?

4. Why is confession so hard for us?

5. How did confession or lack of confession affect the following people? Form four groups, and have each group take one of these passages:
   - *Adam and Eve—Genesis 3:1-19*
   - *Cain—Genesis 4:8-16*
   - *David—2 Samuel 12:1-15; Psalm 51*
   - *The Prodigal Son—Luke 15:11-24*

6. Read the definitions of the word *confess* in the margin. Then look at the way the word *confess* is used in the following verses. Discuss all that it means to confess.
   - *Romans 10:9-10*
   - *Philippians 2:9-11*
   - *Hebrews 13:15*

   > **Confess:**
   > **1** *a)* to admit (a fault or crime)
   > *b)* to acknowledge (an opinion or view)
   > **2** to declare one's faith in.
   >
   > *Webster's New World College Dictionary*

7. Confession can be described as "laying your soul bare" before God. How does being completely open and honest before God affect us and our relationship with God?

Session 3 • Confession

Read Psalm 51:6.

8. Why does God want us to acknowledge the truth about him? the truth about ourselves?

9. How would incorporating confession in your prayers improve your prayer life?

Close It *(15-30 minutes)*

Review the options in the Live It section of this session, and make plans as a group to complete one of these activities prior to moving on to the next session. This is your opportunity to move from theory to practice—*carpe diem!*

Pray It

Share prayer requests, and close in prayer. Be sure to ask God to guide your efforts as you plan and carry out a Live It activity.

Plan It

What activity are we going to do?

When are we doing this?

Where will this take place?

Other: special instructions/my responsibility

Prayer Requests

Part 2: live it

Option 1

Have each group member concentrate on confession in his or her personal prayer life this week. Each day bring your confessions to God concerning a different area of your life. Here is a suggested schedule:

Monday—confess how you have hurt other family members.

Tuesday—confess where you have failed to love your neighbors.

Wednesday—confess where you have failed to live up to Jesus' standards at work, at school, or in your interactions with the business community.

Thursday—confess where you have fallen short in seeking to learn more about God and God's will.

Friday—confess where you have fallen short in your personal morality.

Saturday—confess a way in which you have put other "gods" before the true God (materialism, pleasing people, personal power).

Sunday—confess any improper attitudes you have found within yourself during worship (preoccupation with how you look to others, hostility toward fellow worshippers).

The purpose of all of this is not to feel bad about all your failures but to take a clear look at them, turn them over to God, and make needed changes.

Option 2

Together, recite the following prayer of confession from *The Book of Common Prayer.* Then have a time of silent, corporate prayer for people to confess their own sins. Then have a time for spoken prayer for people to confess aloud what God moves them to confess.

"Almighty and most merciful Father; We have erred, and strayed from thy ways like lost sheep. We have followed too much the devices and desires of our own hearts. We have offended against thy holy laws. We have left undone those things which we ought to have done; And we have done those things which we ought not to have done; And there is no health in us. But thou, O Lord, have mercy upon us, miserable offenders. Spare thou those, O God, who confess their faults. Restore thou those who are penitent; According to thy promises declared unto mankind In Christ Jesus our Lord. And grant,

O most merciful Father, for his sake; That we may hereafter live a godly, righteous, and sober life, To the glory of thy holy Name. Amen."

Option 3

In a journal, start writing all the things you have done that you regret. Don't stop to analyze or censor what you are writing—just write. Then, in your prayer time for the week, take your journal and pray over what you have written. When you see something there for which you need understanding, ask for understanding from God. When you see something for which you need forgiveness, ask for forgiveness.

Option 4

Think of one person you have hurt or offended in the past few weeks. Determine what you did that was wrong or inappropriate. First confess it to God in prayer, asking for better understanding of your actions and forgiveness for what you did wrong. Then go to the person, confess, and ask for that person's forgiveness. Make sure that you simply ask for forgiveness—do not try to justify your action or prod the person into confessing how he or she may have wronged you.

Option 5

Together, read parts of *The Confessions of Saint Augustine*. If no one in the group owns a copy, it can be found at the library. There are also several online versions.

Then have everyone work on writing his or her own confession of faith. Read aloud your confessions to one another. Then pray together, confessing your faith in God and the truth about yourselves.

Debrief It

After experiencing this session's Live It activity, discuss these questions as a group:

- **On a scale of 1 (low) to 10 (high), how would you rank this experience for yourself? Why?**
- **What was the most important insight you gained from this experience?**
- **How can you incorporate this kind of prayer into your life regularly?**

Journal It

The following space is provided for you to record your personal thoughts, reflections, impressions, or feelings about this session's topic and Live It activity.

SESSION 4

Petition

To petition God is to ask God to do something or to give us something. It's the kind of prayer with which everyone who has ever prayed is familiar, whether or not he or she is Christian. Asking God to help us or to protect us or to bless us seems to come naturally. We may occasionally feel guilty for always asking God for this or that, but God tells us to ask him for what we need. We may feel guilty or think we're being selfish. But the Bible tells us that God is a loving Father who enjoys giving good gifts to his children.

While God delights in hearing our petitions, this does not mean that prayer is all about *what I want*. God's desire is to deepen our relationship with him by sharing in what concerns us, just as a good earthly father would. Making our petitions known to God promotes two-way communication. We actively make him part of our struggles and desires in the hope of finding the best answers for our lives. This lesson will help you understand why God is eager for us to make requests of him. You'll see how petitioning God affects our relationship with him and how it helps us to foster a sense of dependence on him and appreciation for all he does for us.

Part 1: *learn it*

Start It *(15 minutes)*
Daily Distractions

Choose one of the following sentences to finish. Share your answer with the group.

- The most bizarre thing anyone ever asked of me was...

- The biggest thing anyone ever asked of me was...

- The most offensive thing anyone ever asked of me was...

- The most unreasonable thing anyone ever asked of me was...

Then discuss these questions:

- How do you feel when someone asks something of you?

- How do you feel when you must ask someone else to do something for you?

- How do you feel about bringing your requests to God?

Study It *(45-60 minutes)*

> If you have a large group, form smaller groups of four to seven people to answer the discussion questions. At the end of the Study It section, allow time for the subgroups to report to the whole group.

1. Do you ever feel uncomfortable or selfish asking God for what you want or need? Why or why not?

Read the quotation from **The Screwtape Letters.**

2. Have you ever fallen into the "heads I win, tails you lose" trap? Explain.

3. What other misconceptions about "unanswered" prayer discourage people from praying or from believing in the power of prayer?

> "Don't forget to use the 'heads I win, tails you lose' argument. If the thing he prays for doesn't happen, then that is one more proof that petitionary prayers don't work; if it does happen, he will, of course, be able to see some of the physical causes which led up to it, and 'therefore it would have happened anyway.'"

Screwtape

Screwtape is the fictional author of The Screwtape Letters, *a book by C.S. Lewis. The book is a collection of letters that Screwtape, an important official in his Satanic Majesty's "Lowerarchy," writes to his nephew Wormwood, a junior devil. The letters seek to encourage Wormwood in his efforts to tempt a human away from becoming a Christian.*

4. What should we believe about how, when, and why God answers our prayers?

Read Matthew 7:7-11.

5. Why does Jesus encourage us to ask God for what we need?

6. What are we to ask God for? Are there things we shouldn't ask for?

Read Luke 18:1-8.

   7. How does this parable teach that we should "always pray and not give up"?

   8. Why does Jesus urge persistence in prayer?

Read James 4:2-3.

   9. What will keep God from giving us what we ask for? What attitude should we have when we petition God?

10. Is it desirable for Christians to be people who continually make requests of God? Why or why not?

11. How does making requests of God affect the way we view ourselves, others, and God?

Close It *(15-30 minutes)*

Review the options in the Live It section of this session, and make plans as a group to complete one of these activities prior to moving on to the next session. This is your opportunity to move from theory to practice—*carpe diem!*

Pray It

Share prayer requests, and close in prayer. Be sure to ask God to guide your efforts as you plan and carry out a Live It activity.

Plan It

What activity are we going to do?

When are we doing this?

Where will this take place?

Other: special instructions/my responsibility

Part 2: live it

Option 1

Plan for an extended time of prayer—at least an hour and up to three or four hours. Gather, being sure to put aside all distractions. Choose several categories for prayer such as church, family, career, purpose, and health. Open your prayer time with praise and thanksgiving, then move into a time of petition. Have one person introduce each category, spreading them out fairly evenly in the time frame you've chosen. Have this same person close the prayer.

Option 2

Provide each person with a box, tape, gift bows, and enough newsprint to wrap the box as if it were a gift. Have each person write John 15:7 on a sheet of paper and place it inside the box. Then have each person wrap his or her box in the newsprint and put a bow on top.

Next, enter into a time of prayer. Have each person consider things for which he or she would like to ask God. Have the group pray aloud as each person feels led. For each request a person makes of God, have him or her write a word or symbol on the box. Close the prayer by thanking God for his answers. Have everyone take home his or her box. The boxes will serve as reminders that God answers prayer.

Option 3

Plan for a time of prayer later this week. Encourage each group member to bring fifteen to twenty verses of Scripture that include a quality or a gift for which he or she would like to ask God or a promise from God he or she would like to ask God to keep. When you gather, decide how long you will pray. Shoot for at least an hour. Make prayer the focus of your time together. Have the group members take turns praying a verse to God and asking God to fulfill that verse in their own lives. Have one person close when time is up.

Option 4

Gather for a time of prayer. Be sure to meet for at least an hour. Everyone will need a note card with this paraphrase of

Matthew 7:11 written on it: "Our Father in heaven gives good gifts to those who ask him." You'll also need a leader who will lead the group in adopting various postures of prayer, such as: sitting with head bowed; kneeling with head bowed and hands clasped; standing with hands outstretched; or standing with hands outstretched, head raised, and eyes open.

Pray together, encouraging people to ask whatever they want of God as they feel moved. As each person finishes a request, have the group respond together, "Our Father in heaven gives good gifts to those who ask him." Periodically, have the leader silently change his or her posture, and have the rest of the group follow his or her lead.

Option 5

Spend several minutes thumbing through several different magazines and newspapers together. Pay specific attention to the advertisements and to what people think they want and are driven to acquire. Tear out the ads and spread them on the floor, then gather around them. For several minutes, consider the ads on the floor as you each consider what you would like to pray about. Consider how your requests are similar to and different from the desires represented in the ads. Consider also the power and wisdom of the one to whom you go with your requests. Then thoughtfully and reverently pray, freely asking God for what you want and need and fully trusting that God will hear your prayers and respond according to his will.

Debrief It

After experiencing this session's Live It activity, discuss these questions as a group:

- **On a scale of 1 (low) to 10 (high), how would you rank this experience for yourself? Why?**

- **What was the most important insight you gained from this experience?**

- **How can you incorporate this kind of prayer into your life regularly?**

Journal It

The following space is provided for you to record your personal thoughts, reflections, impressions, or feelings about this session's topic and Live It activity.

SESSION 5

Intercession

To intercede is to make a request on another's behalf. To pray a prayer of intercession is to pray for someone else. A couple of news stories show the public's interest in intercessory prayer and its fascination with the idea that God might actually be listening.

A few years ago, researchers suggested that prayer might help open-heart surgery patients heal. Researchers suggested a scientific test for prayer: Some patients would be prayed for, and others would not, and researchers would track the results. Some people felt the results indicated that those who were prayed for did heal better and more quickly. Others felt the study was flawed. Some Christians questioned the appropriateness of such a study.

Nuns in New York and New Jersey also made the news for their "Adopt-A-Sister" program. Send in a cash donation, and a nun would pray for you for one year. The nuns were seeking to raise money for a new facility. They said donors were not "buying prayer"; the nuns would pray for anyone who requested prayer, whether or not the person donated money.

Clearly, people are interested in intercessory prayer. For Christians, intercession is to be a regular part of our conversations with God. By command and example, Scripture tells us that we are to pray for others. It is both a privilege and a responsibility. And Christians can be certain that God hears our prayers and will answer according to his will.

This lesson will help you understand more about praying for others. It will also help you put into practice what you've learned by giving you the opportunity to pray for your family, your friends, and your community.

Part 1: *learn it*

Start It *(15 minutes)*
Answered Prayer

Tell the group about one of the following situations in your life:

- a time you prayed for someone and how God answered the prayer

- a time someone prayed for you and how God answered the prayer

- a time you prayed for someone and were uncertain about God's answer

- a time someone prayed for you and you were uncertain about God's answer

Then discuss your reaction to the two examples of intercessory prayer mentioned in the introduction to the lesson.

Study It *(45-60 minutes)*

> If you have a large group, form smaller groups of four to seven people to answer the discussion questions. At the end of the **Study It** section, allow time for the subgroups to report to the whole group.

1. Why does God want us to pray for others?

Read the margin note.

2. What does intercessory prayer do for us? for the people for whom we pray?

3. What should we ask God to do for others?

Read Isaiah 53:12 and Hebrews 7:24-25.

4. How does Christ intercede for us? How is that similar to and different from how we intercede for others?

> "I commend the blessed privilege of intercession, because of its sweet brotherly nature. You and I may be naturally hard, and harsh, and unlovely of spirit, but praying much for others will remind us we have, indeed, a relationship to the saints, that their interests are ours, that we are jointly concerned with them in all the privileges of grace. I do not know anything which, through the grace of God, may be a better means of uniting us the one to the other than constant prayer for each other."
>
> **Charles Spurgeon**

Read 1 Samuel 12:23.

5. Do you consider intercession to be a sacred duty? Explain.

6. Is any Christian exempted from being an intercessor? Do some have a special gift for intercession? Explain.

7. Form pairs or trios. Have each pair or trio look up one or two of the following Scripture passages and note the principles of intercession. After three or four minutes, have each pair or trio summarize its passages and share insights with the rest of the group.

- *Matthew 5:44*
- *2 Corinthians 1:10-11*
- *Ephesians 6:18-20*
- *Philippians 1:18b-19*
- *Colossians 1:9-12*
- *Colossians 4:12*
- *1 Timothy 2:1-4*

8. What can we expect God to do when we pray for others?

9. Is interceding for others a priority in your prayer life? Why or why not?

Read the margin note.

10. What can you do to become more of an intercessor?

> "Brethren, again I say I would earnestly exhort you to intercede for others, for how can you be Christians if you do not? Christians are priests, but how priests if they offer no sacrifice? Christians are lights, but how lights unless they shine for others? Christians are sent into the world, even as Christ was sent into the world, but how sent unless they are sent to pray? Christians are meant not only to be blessed themselves, but in them shall all the nations of the earth be blessed, but how if you refuse to pray?"
>
> **Charles Spurgeon**

Close It *(15-30 minutes)*

Review the options in the Live It section of this session, and make plans as a group to complete one of these activities prior to moving on to the next session. This is your opportunity to move from theory to practice—*carpe diem!*

Pray It

Share prayer requests, and close in prayer. Be sure to ask God to guide your efforts as you plan and carry out a Live It activity.

Plan It

What activity are we going to do?

When are we doing this?

Where will this take place?

Other: special instructions/my responsibility

Part 2: live it

Option 1

Exchange names within the group, and be prayer partners for the next week. Take time to talk with your prayer partner and find specific ways you can pray for him or her. Then make a commitment to pray for your prayer partner throughout each day.

Option 2

Together, make a list of people and situations for which you would like to pray, and be as detailed and complete as possible. Then plan for an extended session of prayer. For example, you may plan to pray for twelve hours (9:00 a.m. to 9:00 p.m.) one Saturday. Meet and pray together for the first and last hour. Divide the other ten hours among the group so that each person will pray during a specific block of time. Make sure that each person has a copy of the prayer list.

Option 3

Choose an area or neighborhood in your town in which you would like to see God work. Form pairs or trios, and have each pair or trio spend one afternoon or evening this week walking through that area or neighborhood, praying for the people who live or work there. If possible, schedule your prayer walks during daylight hours. Also take whatever safety precautions you feel are necessary.

As each pair or trio walks, have group members pay attention to their surroundings and to the people they see. If you're praying through a neighborhood, pray for the people who live in each home. Pray for those you see outdoors. Pray for situations that arise during your walk. For example, you might hear arguments, or you might see children who need attention or supervision. Pray that God would be at work in the neighborhood and that the residents would desire to seek God and be drawn into relationship with him. Pray that Christians in the neighborhood would be strengthened in their faith and would be called to reach their neighbors with the gospel. Pray that churches in the neighborhood would be healthy and strong.

Option 4

Together as a group, find an organization that has an intercessory prayer program and sign up. For example, Wycliffe has a program through which you can pray for people groups that do not yet have the Bible in their own language. Check it out at www.wycliffe.org. The Voice of the Martyrs is another organization that has an intercessory prayer program—www.persecution.com. Pray regularly for the people in the organization you choose.

Option 5

Conduct a prayer walk through your church the day before services are held. Have your group split up and wander through the church, praying for your church's ministries. Have someone stand behind the pulpit and pray for the pastor and the message he or she will give to the congregation. Stand where the musicians stand, and pray for them to lead the church in worshipping God. Sit where the congregation sits, and pray that they will be encouraged to worship God in spirit and in truth and that they will be encouraged and challenged in their faith. Pray in the nursery; pray in each staff member's office; pray in each classroom; pray in the kitchen; pray in the playground; pray in the parking lot. Be sure to pray for teachers, for those who attend the church, for families, for children, for the youth, and for those who will visit the church. Pray for those who are strong in their faith, and pray for those who need encouragement. Pray for those who are going through tough times.

Your group may want to do this every week. Or you may want to enlist the help of other Bible study groups and take turns so that your church's ministries and members are prayed for every week.

Debrief It

After experiencing this session's Live It activity, discuss these questions as a group:

- **On a scale of 1 (low) to 10 (high), how would you rank this experience for yourself? Why?**

- **What was the most important insight you gained from this experience?**

- **How can you incorporate this kind of prayer into your life regularly?**

Journal It

The following space is provided for you to record your personal thoughts, reflections, impressions, or feelings about this session's topic and Live It activity.

SESSION 6

Listening to God

In this series of lessons on prayer, we have learned that talking to God is an important part of prayer. But talking isn't all there is to prayer. Prayer is also about us listening to God. The idea that God speaks to us raises all sorts of questions. How does God speak? Is it only through Scripture? Does God ever speak in an audible voice? How can we be sure that what we're hearing is from God? Is it presumptuous for one to say, "God told me..."?

These questions aren't the only problems for us when we consider listening to God. Too often, Christians think that God only speaks to the spiritually elite. But God desires an intimate relationship with us. Part of developing intimacy is learning how to develop an ongoing conversation with God. You can be confident that God has something to say to you! This lesson will help you understand how God speaks to his children, and it will give you a chance to practice listening to what he has to say to you.

Part 1: learn it

Start It *(15 minutes)*
Learning to Listen

To get things started today, play one round of the game Telephone. Sit in a circle, and choose someone to go first. Have that person think up a phrase and whisper it to the person on his or her right. That person whispers what he or she heard to the person on his or her right, and the phrase gets passed all the way around the circle. Have the last person say the phrase aloud. Is the phrase the same, or did it change as it was passed from person to person?

Then talk about how this game is like or unlike listening to God.

Next, choose one of these sentences to complete and share with the group:

- **The one time I was sure God was speaking to me was...**

- **The thing that confuses me the most about listening to God is...**

- **The strangest thing that I heard someone say God told them was...**

Study It *(45-60 minutes)*

> If you have a large group, form smaller groups of four to seven people to answer the discussion questions. At the end of the Study It section, allow time for the subgroups to report to the whole group.

Read Isaiah 30:21.

1. Do you feel that God speaks to you? If not, why do you think that is? If so, tell the group one example of the "what, where, when, why, and how" of God's messages to you.

Read the quotation from Francis Schaeffer.

2. Is it possible for God to speak to us and for us not to hear or understand what God says? Explain.

3. Why is listening an important part of prayer?

> "The personal God has made us to speak to each other in language. So if a personal God has made us to be language communicators—and that is obviously what man is—why then should it be surprising to think of him speaking to Paul in Hebrew on the Damascus Road? Why should it be a surprise? Do we think God does not know Hebrew?"
>
> **Francis Schaeffer,** *He Is There and He Is Not Silent*

Session 6 • Listening to God

4. What do you think it means to listen to God? When are we to do that? How are we to do that?

Read Luke 10:38-41.

5. Are you more like Mary or Martha when it comes to listening to God?

6. What gets in the way of listening to God? What helps us listen to God?

Read 1 Kings 19:9-13.

7. In what ways do you identify with Elijah's encounter with God? When do you expect to hear from God? Have you been surprised by his voice?

8. How can we become more attentive to that still, small voice and more willing to respond?

Read 1 Samuel 3:1-10.

9. In what ways do you identify with Samuel's encounter with God? What does this passage teach you about listening to God?

Read Luke 6:49.

10. What can you do to heed this warning?

11. How would your life be affected if you spent more time listening to God? What steps can you take to listen to God more?

Close It *(15-30 minutes)*

Review the options in the Live It section of this session, and make plans as a group to complete one of these activities prior to moving on to the next session. This is your opportunity to move from theory to practice—*carpe diem!*

Pray It

Share prayer requests, and close in prayer. Be sure to ask God to guide your efforts as you plan and carry out a Live It activity.

Plan It

What activity are we going to do?

When are we doing this?

Where will this take place?

Other: special instructions/my responsibility

Part 2: live it

Option 1

Gather for at least an hour of complete silence, and listen to God together. Make sure phones, radios, and televisions are turned off. This would be a good week for children to be taken care of at another location. Do your best to minimize all interruptions. Have everyone find a comfortable place to sit. Provide everyone with a glass of water, take bathroom breaks before you start, and have tissues handy. Make sure that each person has a Bible. Be warned though: It would be easy to spend the hour reading rather than listening to God, so only use the Bible if God specifically directs you to Scripture. Some people may also want to have paper and a pen. At the end of the hour, share your insights with each other.

Option 2

Choose one day this week to have everyone spend purposefully listening to God as you all go about your daily business. This is a day to truly "pray without ceasing." Ask God what he wants you to do as soon as you wake. Ask God to make you aware of his blessings as you drive the kids to school or go to work. Ask God to point out people you can encourage or to whom you can minister as you go through your day. Do each task reverently and prayerfully. Ask God to direct your every step. Ask God to show you his purposes for you. Write down what God tells you, and be ready to share it with the group when you next meet.

Option 3

Meet together for at least an hour outdoors. Choose a park that isn't near traffic and that isn't crowded with people. Walk around the park, letting each person wander where he or she would like. Listen carefully to the sounds around you. Notice the sounds that you're aware of immediately. Notice how much more you hear as time passes and you become more focused and aware of your surroundings. Use all of your senses in the same way: What do you see? What do you feel? What do you smell? After spending ten or fifteen minutes becoming fully aware of your surroundings, turn your attention to God. Listen carefully to him. Use your senses to become aware of his voice. Be ready to tell your group your insights.

Option 4

Gather for a time of meditation. Plan for at least thirty minutes. Have each person bring a verse about God that has particular meaning to him or her. For example, someone might choose Isaiah 53:7, "He was oppressed and afflicted, yet he did not open his mouth; he was led like a lamb to the slaughter, and as a sheep before her shearers is silent, so he did not open his mouth."

Have each person silently focus on his or her verse. One way to do this is simply to repeat the verse several times as a prayer. Another way to do this is to consider the meaning of each word and each phrase slowly, asking God to meet with you and to speak to you through his Word. This isn't a time for active prayer about your own concerns; it's a time to sit, listen, and wait for God. As thoughts wander or the cares of the world intrude, gently return to the verse and focus on God. Don't be surprised if you become unusually restless or aware of pains or itches. Don't let these physical things distract you—simply put such cares out of your mind and refocus your attention on Scripture and God.

This can be a powerfully emotional time. Don't be surprised if you are moved to tears.

Have someone pay attention to the time—you may want to set an alarm. At the end of the time, remain in silence for a minute or two to allow people to finish their time of meditation and prepare to "re-enter" the regular world.

Option 5

Together, create a prayer path in someone's backyard or basement.

Prayer paths (or labyrinths) have been used for hundreds of years to help people focus more intently on God. Historically, a prayer path or labyrinth is a winding path that moves inward to a center and then back out to the starting point. As walkers move reverently and prayerfully toward the center, they leave behind the cares and distractions of the world and become more aware of

God's presence. At the center, they spend time communing intimately with God and listening to his wise counsel. As the walkers move outward, they consider how their encounter with God will transform their lives.

You can use the illustration in the margin as a guide to build your labyrinth. It's an illustration of the Chartes Cathedral Labyrinth at Chartes, Frances. Or you can use any shape you want. You can mark your path with small stones, with masking tape, or with chalk. Place pillows, Bibles, and communion elements at the center.

Once the prayer path is built, plan on a time for the group to gather and walk it. This should be done silently, slowly, and reverently. If possible, take off your shoes to show your reverence. Have people begin walking the path at five-minute intervals. When people reach the center, encourage them to linger with God, reading Scripture, listening to God, and taking communion before they begin the journey outward.

Debrief It

After experiencing this session's Live It activity, discuss these questions as a group:

- On a scale of 1 (low) to 10 (high), how would you rank this experience for yourself? Why?

- What was the most important insight you gained from this experience?

- How can you incorporate this kind of prayer into your life regularly?

Journal It

The following space is provided for you to record your personal thoughts, reflections, impressions, or feelings about this session's topic and Live It activity.

learn it live it

SESSION 7

The Lord's Prayer

If you did a simple search on the Internet for "The Lord's Prayer," you could end up with close to 400,000 Web sites through which to browse! Songs have been written about it, believers are comforted by it, churches recite it, governments have removed it from their buildings, school boards have banned students from publicly praying it, Christians of different denominations have disagreed over its use, and Todd Beamer recited it with a supervisor from the GTE Customer Center just before confronting hijackers on September 11, 2001. Why all the attention? Scripture itself indicates that Jesus' disciples asked him how they should pray. This prayer was Jesus' answer to their question.

In this final lesson on prayer, you'll take an in-depth look at the Lord's Prayer. You'll explore Jesus' intent when he gave this prayer to his disciples, and you'll consider its place in a Christian's daily life. Then you'll bring the prayer and the principles behind it into your daily life so that your conversations with God become even more intimate.

Part 1: learn it

Start It *(15 minutes)*
Parent Talk

To begin today's lesson, remember what your relationship was like with one of your parents when you were a teenager. Think specifically about what it was like to have a conversation with that parent. Circle all the words below that apply. Be ready to share with the group what it was like to talk to your parent.

When I was a teenager, conversation with my parent was:

Fun	Halting	Rewarding	Casual
Awkward	Truthful	Nonexistent	Respectful
Easy	Formal	Frequent	Rebellious
Painful	Productive	Helpful	Evasive

Then choose one or two of the following questions to answer and share with the group:

- What was the most significant conversation you ever had with your parent?

- What was the most significant conversation you ever had with God?

- How does talking to God, your Father in heaven, compare to talking with your parent?

Study It *(45-60 minutes)*

> If you have a large group, form smaller groups of four to seven people to answer the discussion questions. At the end of the Study It section, allow time for the subgroups to report to the whole group.

Read Matthew 6:5-8. Also read the margin note.

> "He who prays as he ought will endeavor to live as he prays."
>
> **John Owen**

1. Why does Jesus give us these warnings? What are we *not* to do when we pray? How should we pray, and what should our attitude be?

2. In light of verses 5-8, why do you think Christians pray the Lord's Prayer rather than using it only as a model for their prayers? Do you think this practice is right or wrong? Explain.

Read Matthew 6:8 again.

3. If God already knows what we need, why do we pray? List as many reasons as you can.

Read Matthew 6:9-13.

4. Jesus says that this is *how* we should pray. What point do you think Jesus was making in giving us this prayer?

5. What principles about prayer can you glean from each verse of Matthew 6:9-13?
Verse 9:

Verse 10:

Verse 11:

Verse 12:

Verse 13:

6. How mindful of all these principles are you when you pray? What do you tend to leave out or focus on too much?

7. Why do you think these are the principles of prayer Jesus felt were important to mention?

8. What do you learn from the way the prayer is arranged? What's listed first? last? Is there a flow of ideas in the prayer?

9. How can you incorporate the principles you've learned about the Lord's Prayer into your prayer life every day?

Close It *(15-30 minutes)*

Review the options in the Live It section of this session, and make plans as a group to complete one of these activities soon. This is your opportunity to move from theory to practice—*carpe diem!*

Pray It

Share prayer requests, and close in prayer. Be sure to ask God to guide your efforts as you plan and carry out a Live It activity.

Since this is the last session in this study, discuss what the group would like to do next. You may want to have a party to celebrate the completion of this course.

Plan It

What activity are we going to do?

When are we doing this?

Where will this take place?

Other: special instructions/my responsibility

Part 2: live it

Option 1

As a group, rewrite the Lord's Prayer in your own words, using contemporary language, metaphors, similes, word pictures, and other techniques to describe the intent of the prayer. You may want to form pairs to do this. To get you started, consider looking up Matthew 6:9-13 in as many Bible versions as you can find. You may want to make your version rhyme, or you may want to set it to music. When you all have finished, pray each version of the Lord's Prayer that you wrote.

Option 2

Gather for a time of corporate prayer, letting the Lord's Prayer be your model. Pray each phrase of the prayer aloud. Then pause to let people add their individual prayers. For example, offer prayers of praise after you pray, "hallowed be your name," and ask God to give you wisdom and guidance after you pray, "your will be done on earth as it is in heaven."

Option 3

Individually, pray the Lord's Prayer for an entire week, putting it in your own words and using it as a model to guide your conversation with God. Or focus on one prayer element from this session for an entire day. For example, your prayer time on Monday might consist of praising God for who he is and what he has done; on Tuesday, you could focus on asking God to do the things that he has promised to do in your life, other people's lives, or the world. Then, the next time your group gathers, report how you and your conversation with God were affected by your guided prayers.

Option 4

Hang five large pieces of poster board around the room. Write one of the five verses of the Lord's Prayer at the top of each piece of poster board. If you would like, add a sixth piece of poster board, and write on it, "For yours is the kingdom and the power and the glory forever. Amen." Place a package of multicolored markers near each piece of poster board. Form five (or six) groups, and have each group stand or sit in front of one of the pieces of poster board. Set a kitchen timer to go off in ten minutes. During that ten minutes, each group will pray individually or corporately about the topic of prayer that's on its piece of poster board. Have group members write words or draw pictures on the piece of poster board to show what they've prayed about. When the timer goes off, have everyone rotate to the next piece of poster board. Set the timer for ten minutes again, and have groups pray about their new topics. Continue until everyone has prayed about all the topics. Then gather and talk about what's written on each piece of poster board.

Option 5

Give everyone a disposable camera. Have everyone pray the Lord's Prayer daily and prayerfully take pictures throughout the week to illustrate each of the verses of the Lord's Prayer. For example, someone might take pictures of ministries that illustrate God's kingdom on earth for the verse "your kingdom come, your will be done on earth as it is in heaven." A typical disposable camera has twenty-seven exposures, so everyone should be able to take about five pictures for each verse. Have group members develop their film before you meet again. Together, recite each verse of the Lord's prayer, pausing after each verse for each person to show his or her "photo essay" on that topic.

Debrief It

After experiencing this session's Live It activity, discuss these questions as a group:

- On a scale of 1 (low) to 10 (high), how would you rank this experience for yourself? Why?

- What was the most important insight you gained from this experience?

- How can you incorporate this kind of prayer into your life regularly?

Journal It

The following space is provided for you to record your personal thoughts, reflections, impressions, or feelings about this session's topic and Live It activity.